Manhattan to Machipongo

Ken Sutton

Poems and writings herein are the products of Ken Sutton, who is responsible for these contents. Wider Perspectives Publishing reserves 1st run of printing rights, but all materials revert to property of the author at time of delivery. All rights to republication of items inside thereafter revert to the author, and he may submit items to contests and anthologies at will.

Credits
"Pumpkin Trees & Acorn Vines", "On First Looking Into Pogo's Ten Everlovin' Blue Eyed Years", & "Last Note on a Unicorn's Horn" first appeared in The Helicon, the literary journal of Northeast Louisiana University, now University of Louisiana, Monroe.

"Pumpkin Trees & Acorn Vines" has also been set to music by Stephan Dulcie and performed by Richard Williams on June 8, 2014.

"The Voice of the Turtle", "Sirens" & "Eastern Shore Traffic Jam" appeared in the anthology *Our Virginia*, in 2017 collected and edited by La Belle Rouge.

"How to Study a Poem" & "Wild Violets" appeared in Chronogram magazine.

"Temporary Repair" was recorded for WHRO November 2017 for broadcast as part of their Writers Block series in 2018.

1st run released 2018 Hampton Roads, Virginia

Copyright Feb. 15, 2018, Kenneth Sutton, Hampton Roads
Wider Perspectives Publishing
1st Ed.2018 ISBN-13: 978-1985618909/ -10: 1985618907
2nd ed. 2020 ISBN: 978-1-952773-13-6

Acknowledgments & Dedication

The photos are by Phillip Spohn. He can be contacted at Phillip Spohn Photography on FB, or phillipspohn on Instagram. He does good work and proved to be flexible to my needs.

In the fall of 2012 I decided to return to poetry on a serious basis. I thank the following for encouraging and goading me along the way.

The writer's workshop at the Eastern Shore's Own Art Center (ESO) in Belle Haven, Virginia run by Lenore Hart and David Poyer. There is nothing like the brutal honesty of a group of fellow writers to hone your work. I recommend their workshop to anyone seeking to better their writing. Just remember to check your ego at the door.

To my all fellow poets, particularly Bob Arthur, Bill Glose, Carolyn Foronda, Jorge Mendez and especially Ann Shalaski. She has provided guidance though the nuts and bolts of birthing a book.

To the PoetCyn, a good friend who has left us. Before going she made me a gift of the phrase "Cleopatra Cleavage". I hope she approves of the use I put it to.

Finally and chiefly to my wife, Carolyn, my biggest fan and most severe critic. She has told me often, "You need to work some more on that one." She has never been wrong.

Manhattan to Machipongo	1
The Arc of Childhood	4
When Stars Fell on Windmill Beach	5
Pumpkin Trees & Acorn Vines	9
Grandfather Bear	20
Kiptopeke's Song to His Son	23
Wendigo	27
Damsel Fly	29
Mortal Sin	30
First Grade Theology	34
In the Beginning	36
Sister Victoria	38
110 North Pleasant Street	39
The Making of Grandfather Frog	40
Listening to Runa	42
Roads Taken	44
The Gravity of the Situation	46
Wakefield	48
New Bedford	50
August in the Berkshires	55
Chipmunk and Granite	56
The Old Men of the Sea	57
Man with a Blown Guitar	58
Coffee after Labor Day	60
Old Men of Chatham	61
Used Book Store	62
Cape Cod Cats	63
Poem of Two Voices	64
Good Is Not Interred	65
Comb	66
Temporary Repair	67
The Geography of Leaves	70
In Memoriam	71
Visiting Doris	72

Magna Cum Latte	73
Parades	75
Sirens	77
Fedoras	79
Waiting for Fish	80
Calico and Gold	81
On the Superiority of Cats	83
The Advantages of Owning a Magician	84
Carpe Diem Redux	87
Wild Violets	88
Buddy Knows His Business	89
Hungars Creek Winter Time Blues	90
Hungars Creek Spring	92
The Voice of the Turtle Is Heard in Our Land	94
Machipongo Mountain Range	97
Machipongo Mist	98
The Old Man of Wachapreague	99
Tangier Isalnd	100
The Company of Cats	101
Coffee at the Machipongo Trading Company	102
A Question I Have Pondered	104
Now and Again	
All Day	107
The Burden of Fame	108
Adonis at Seventy-Three	110
Donnie's Guitar	112
Cleopatra Cleavage	114
Life after Death	116
Carneys Before the Dawn	117
A Violin Played	118
The Vatic Frog	119
Rejection Letter	120
From Dr. Seuss's Publisher	
Trust	121

On First Looking Into	122
Pogo's Ten Everlovin' Blue Eyed Years	
I like a lot of milk in my coffee.	123
The Genealogy of Hotdogs	125
Eastern Shore Traffic Jam	126
October's Dance	128
Let Us Go Then You and I	129
Mattawoman Flats	130
Chuck Willow	131
Monarch of All She Surveys	132
Winter Kingfisher	133
First Fire	134
Ax and Wood	135
Wood Heat	136
Punctuation	139
Quotidian	142
Mixology	143
How to Study a Poem	144
Last Note on a Unicorns Horn	146

Manhattan to Machipongo

While the postmistress searches for
a small green man carving
shipped from Thibodaux Louisiana
somewhere in the pale brown jumble
of rectangle and cubes,
I flip through my New Yorker,
checking out the cartoons.

I notice that the address label is MIA.
Somewhere between its last Zip Code sort
and Machipongo, duty almost done,
it fell to enemy action, ripped from the cover,
its frail body tucked in some cranny
of the automated sorting machines in Richmond.

Or maybe it just went AWOL,
fluttering about a drafty mail truck,
plotting its escape with a Dixie cup.

So how did she know the magazine was mine,
I ask, exchanging question for parcel.

"You're the only one from New York City."
I hail from the orchards, cider mills,
and rock strewn trout streams
of upstate, almost Canada, New York,
from Watertown, the Little Apple.

I've long stopped explaining the Saint Lawrence River
does not flow through the boroughs of Gotham
and the Thousand Islands do not speckle Central Park's lakes.
I think she just likes pulling my come-here leg.

The real answer of course; Machipongo is small.
(The post office lobby would barely make spec

for a seven by ten federal prison cell.)
She knows all her box holder's mail by heart.

Home, I take my coffee and mail to the sun porch,
feed the stove's bed of coals a ration of red oak
and admire Hickory Cove, a slender arm
of Chesapeake Bay that nudges its way
into our back yard and its attendant marsh,
tawny winter reeds shedding pale frost sheaths.
(Only nature would think to silver plate gold
or so thoughtlessly undo her own effort.)

One blue heron sits on a piling of my neighbors dock
patiently waiting for the rising tide to fracture
last night's thin ice, shove it out of the way,
and let him get to the earnest matter of breakfast.

When I burrow past The New Yorker's cartoons
into "The Talk of the Town" I discover
a practical, if odd, unit of measure,
the Manhattan Cord, 40 cubic feet of wood,
kiln dried and shrink wrapped.

Its consumers are wealthy apartment dwellers
and restaurateurs that advertize wood fired ovens.
You could hardly run a standard cord,
with its litter of bark and bugs,
through the halls of Trump Tower.

And where in a pizzeria's kitchen would you park
a hundred twenty eight dirty cubic feet?

But slip a clean Manhattan Cord on a two wheeled dolly
and you can navigate arrogant elevators,
and spotless restaurants without complaint,
a true servant of its environment.

It would never do here, where wood is not fuel
for restaurant ovens and living room conversations,
but the serious matter of warming a house and two cats.

My stove takes fourteen inch wood
and I stack it just short of shoulder high
between trees near the house,
that, for no reason beyond chance,
stand about sixteen feet apart.

I have decided to call this unit, the Machipongo Cord.
I think I'll mention it next time I'm at the post office.
Give me something to talk about when I pick up my mail.
Give her something to talk about when I leave.

The Arc of Childhood

For reasons lost in the logic of childhood
I once spent an entire Saturday morning
covering our car with a thick coat of sand.

I lugged my sandbox into the garage
one bucket at a time and layered it on,
dampening it carefully to make it stick.

Dad spent his afternoon displacing my effort,
letting it fall to the concrete for me to sweep up
and trundle back to my wood framed desert.

Later, the one grain he missed etched an arc
on the passenger side of the windshield
that gleamed like a scythe when it caught the sun.

At night when the taillights hit it
the scythe flickered red, bleeding,
like the Genesee sign at Jasper's Tavern.

Coming back from Westcott's Beach
the moon, racing alongside our green Hudson,
would flame the scythe with soft silver.

I could almost believe
that it wouldn't cut me
if I touched it, almost.

When Stars Fell on Windmill Beach

Camping and five, I watched my father
dive for starfish at Windmill Beach.
He decorated the low tide strand
with star patterns, big dipper and little.

The dippers are really bears with tails.
If you would like to hear how the bear
lost his tail, fetch my pipe and tobacco.

He set Sir Walter Raleigh smoldering,
blew two clouds of smoke into the air,
set a third swirling when he spoke,

In the before times...

>The fox and bear were proud of their tails.
>Each held his the most glorious in the woodland.
>
>Some agreed with the fox,
>said he carried a dancing plume of fire,
>that lit the world wherever he went.
>
>Some favored the bear,
>marveled at his extraordinarily long tail,
>black and shiny as a river under moonlight.
>
>Each thought his tail the best.
>Each feared the other's might be better.
>
>Late one bitter winter afternoon
>the bear chanced upon the fox
>coming across a frozen lake,
>a ring perch in his mouth.

How did a little runt like you,
a mere fox, catch such a tasty fish?

The fox laid the perch on the ice
and pinned it with his paw
to remind the bear that it was his.

With my beautiful tail.
He flicked it back and forth
like a furry flame.
A tail like yours, Noble Bear,
could catch Grandfather Pike.

If you don't want to tell me,
just say so. No need to lie.
I'm not stupid, you know.

But the fox knew the bear was stupid.
Just a little, but it would be enough.

Surely, Noble Bear,
you've heard of ice fishing.
In the center of the lake
there is a hole in the ice.
Stick your luxuriant tail in.
When it goes numb,
Grandfather Pike is circling.
When you feel a sharp tingle,
he has tangled his teeth
in your lustrous, beautiful fur.
Yank quickly and pull hard.
Grandfather Pike is long as your tail
and nearly as big around as me.

Course I've heard of ice fishing.
We bears do it all the time.
And big around as a fox
is not very big at all.

The bear trotted off toward the setting sun
and the center of the lake.
The fox munched his ring perch
and watched the bear grow smaller.

The bear found the hole in the ice,
just where the fox said it would be.
When he lowered his tail in the water,
it went numb, just as the fox said it would.

He waited as the moon rose against the dark
and wondered if Grandfather Pike would ever strike,
but then came a sharp tingle,
just as the fox said it would.

He dug his claws in the ice and heaved
to jerk that fish right out of the water.

When he whipped around he saw no pike,
glistening silver under the moon,
only fresh frozen ice gleamed back at him.
He looked for his tail, but found only a nub.

The bear wept over the loss
of his precious ebony river of pride,
shedding one large crystalline tear
and one small shining drop of sorrow.

His tears froze in the air as they fell.
Each shattered on the ice
into seven chips of frigid fire
that sailed off into the dark sea we call sky.

All tears dry in time,
yet these glitter still,
as they have from the before times
and will until tomorrows are no more.

>   For every night when the bear looks up
>   and sees in the stars what he lost on earth
>   he cries the dippers bright again.

Done with his tale,
my father knocked dottle from his pipe
and spun his starfish constellations back into the water,
creating a meteor shower to startle scuttling crabs.

I lay that night tentless,
under a black dome pierced with light.
Found and named the Bear, the Fox
the Ring Perch, even Grandfather Pike.

Bent the Milky Way into a bridge
to save the animals Noah left behind,
Unicorns, and Gryphons, every animal
my father had ever fabled a story with.

Before I slept I saw three stars fall,
startling cars scuttling along
the highway miles from the beach
in a world I would never return to.

**PUMPKIN TREES
&
ACORN VINES**
(A Thrice Told Tale)

When I was a younger child
than I am now

I wondered why acorns
grew on oak trees
and pumpkins
grew on pumpkin vines.

After all
pumpkin vines are so small
and pumpkins so large
while oak trees are so large
and acorns so small.

The conclusion was obvious:
Pumpkins should grow on oak trees
and
acorns should grow on pumpkin vines.

Giving us
pumpkin trees
and
acorn vines.

I presented my conclusion
to Sister Mary Elephant
who told me a story
      (A parable as it were.)
About a young man
      (About my age.)
who was of the same opinion,

Until

One day

He took a nap under an oak tree.

After a while an acorn fell on him and woke him up.

When he realized what woke him up
he reconsidered his conclusion,

accepted reality,

and later,

went on to become a stock broker.

      (And a very successful one I might add.)

Sister Mary Elephant's story
    (A parable as it were.)
satisfied my apprehensions.

I MEAN

        If God screwed up
        such a simple matter as
        oak trees and pumpkin vines

    Then,

        WHAT ELSE?

But

Sister Mary Elephant's story
         (A parable as it were.)
satisfied my apprehensions

Until recently.

Recently it occurred to me,

that anyone stupid enough
to take a nap under a pumpkin tree
got exactly what he deserved
and probably would not be missed.

Grandfather Bear

Sometimes, in the evening,
when I sit on that small concrete slab
that juts out from my carport,
like the jetties that men build
to stop the sea from taking back
the beach it gave and regretted giving,
that small concrete slab I only call a porch,
the wind blows strong enough
and soft enough
to quiet this white man city,
        and
I remember Grandfather Bear.

                *

In the time,

when tree, lake and mountain wore our names
and the white man begged permission to walk our land
and we did not yet know that he was many,

when the river ran clear and turned no wheel
and thickened and darkened
only in the time of the salmon and the smelt,

Grandfather Bear was not Grandfather Bear,
but Young Minnow,
and lived in a longhouse by the river.

                *

In the time of the smelt,
we fished alone.

In the time of the salmon,
the bear fished also.

*

In the time of the smelt,
Young Minnow fished
the chill spring nights
in the ice rimmed river
with the women and children
and the other not-yet-men
as near the fall as was permitted.
The men did not fish at all.
Nor did the bear.

In the time of the salmon,
the men fished on the fall.
The women and children fished
in the clear pool below.
Young Minnow and the other not-yet-men
fished in the whitewater between.
The bear fished where he pleased.

*

Young Minnow caught a great salmon in the whitewater.
He held it proud high and all the women and not-yet-men saw.
Some of the men on the fall saw and smiled.

Young Minnow carried his great salmon high up on the bank
and laid it in the shade of a tree and killed it with a sharp rock.

Young Minnow started down the bank.
The men on the fall began to laugh and point.
Young Minnow turned and saw a big black bear.
The bear was stealing his salmon.

Young Minnow shouted anger and began to climb.
The bear dropped to all four
and, with the great salmon in his mouth,

ran into the woods, Young Minnow chasing after.

Young Minnow chased the bear until the sun fell.
Young Minnow chased the bear until the moon rose.
Young Minnow chased the bear until the moon fell.

Young Minnow never caught the bear,
but was given his man name
and thereafter, fished on the fall.

Kiptopeke's Song to His Son

Father, what holds up the sky?

>The sky rests on the water, my son.
>to the North, South and West,
>it rests on pillars of water.
>
>If you cross the land between bitter water
>and look to the East, where the Sun rises,
>you will find the fourth pillar.

Father, why does the water
not sink under the burden of the sky?

>Not all things are meant to be known.
>We live in mystery, as the bird in the air.

Father, what is the Sun?

>It is the eternal fire that cannot be quenched.
>It rises out of the Eastern bitter water
>and settles in the Western bitter water.
>
>Those who see this for the first time
>think the Sun is born each day
>and goes out at night like a camp fire.
>This is not so.

Father, what is so?

>The sun is like a flicker on the water.
>Your eye sees it where it is not.
>The sun is not truly as we see it.

Father, what then, is the Moon?

> A most strange thing, my son,
> almost beyond belief.
> It is a great fire of white flame
> held in a stone conch shell
> by a thin man with a fat belly
> slowly turning in place.
>
> When he holds the fire in front,
> the night is for hunting.
> When he turns his back,
> the sea fills our nets with fish.
>
> When he turns to the side
> there is not enough light for the hunt,
> but enough that the fish see our nets.
> It is an ill time.
>
> He has always been in the sky,
> slowly turning, holding his fire.
> Some say he is brother to the Sun.
> I do not know if this is true.

Father, what of the Earth?

> The Earth is our mother.
> This is why, when our people die,
> we split the soil to return the dead
> to the womb of their mother.
>
> The Earth is always with us holding us up.
> When we go upon the water
> she holds the water up,
> even as the water holds up our canoe.

Father, how can this be?

>We know that this has always been so,
>but we have never understood it.
>Not all things are meant to be known.
>We live in mystery, as the fish in the sea.

Who then, is our father?

>The Sun is our father and father to all things.
>He has sprayed his seed across the sky,
>and when one of his seed falls upon the earth
>our mother swells and brings forth new life.
>
>This is how it is that you sometimes find
>a new animal, a new bird, or a new fish.
>They do not come from far lands or strange waters.
>They come from Mother Earth and Father Sun.

Father, the white man,
who comes into our creeks
with wide canoes
that spider stride on the water,
is he a new thing?

>He is a new thing
>made to punish us
>for our selfishness.
>That is why he does evil.

Father,
who will punish
the white man
for what he does.

>This is not known. We live in mystery,
>as the fish in the sea, as the bird in the air.
>Indeed, not all things were meant to be known.

But I have seen that the white man soils himself
like an unweaned child. We shall wait.
Perhaps he will learn wisdom. Perhaps we will.

Wendigo

My grandfather told me the Bear
understood every tongue of man,
even the grunting of white men,
but would not speak for sorrow
at Glooskap's betrayal.

He warned me of the Beaver,
who sold Glooskap's life
to his brother Maslum
for the promise of wings
and was betrayed in turn.

"You do not need wings to fly." laughed Maslum,
speaker of truth, teller of lies,
and he kicked the Beaver through the air
from the high bank into the water.

Now she repents her days
in shame below the water,
coming out only at night to fell trees
because they reach for a sky
she still hungers for,

never seeing beyond Maslum's lie
to her own part in her betrayal,
never caring what falling trees crush,
only that they fall.

He terrified me before sleep
with tales of Wendigo
who walked at night
and fed men fear.

When fear made them small
taught them to lust for anger,
to believe in its strength.

And when men's hearts grew fat
in their corruption,
Wendigo ate their souls.

Now I am a man and I know
the bear is a beast
of indifferent intelligence,
that there is no malice or shame
in the heart of the beaver.

But Wendigo?
He is real.

Damselfly

Glittering in the stark sun
it rose out of the reeds
of Kingsbury Pond, flew toward me,
then settled on the last green blade.

I had never seen a damselfly,
never seen such an alive blue,
metallic, as were the cars
I watched from the porch
of my old house on State Street.
But they never shimmered in the light so,
nor moved with such surety of purpose.

"That's the Devil's Darning Needle."
My Grandmother spoke softly behind me.
She had a silent tread.
"God uses it to sew up the lips
of little boys that lie."

At issue was a brownie,
not the last, but the penultimate.
No matter, there were two
where now there was but one.

I had denied all knowledge
and slipped out the kitchen door.
But conscience pursued me
with a quick quiet step

and hushed insinuation.
Twice more I denied,
but lived all that summer
in dread of the damselfly.

Mortal Sin

I had met my grandmother twice
on pilgrimage to her house,
big, rambling, with a disheveled yard,
the first floor sprinkled with Victorian furniture,
the second furnished with echoes
and yellowed lace curtains
on the front windows only.

Now she was coming to live with us, forever.
And it would be just wonderful. Mom said so.
Her voice was a bit brittle,
but, like a bluegill rising to a grasshopper,
I believed. My mother never lied.

Short, slender, barring thick piano legs.
Her grey hair, neatly bunned, green eyes
behind sparkling octagonal wire rims
removed when serious words had to be said.

Granny taught me sin, mortal and venial.

Venial sins you could stack all day, for years,
and not make a mortal sin, not even one.
Young boys, even good little boys,
committed several, at least three, each day.

God forgave venial sin on apology.
If you forgot, missed an I'm sorry,
or perhaps, as even good little boys will,
sinned unaware? Well, purgatory.
And what's a few years in purgatory
against eternal salvation?

Mortal sin could not be forgiven,
save by the good offices of Holy Mother Church

and regular visits to Father Vincent
in the Friday night confessional booth.

Unforgiven mortal sin killed the soul.
But not so dead it could not burn.
No water could quench hellfire, nor ease the pain.
Better a little fire now than eternal agony.

Do you know what quench means, young man?
Eternal? And agony? Here, give me your hand.

See, that was only two seconds.
Hell is God's justice, hotter than any stove
and never stops burning. Not ever.
This piece of aloe is like Christ.
Cutting and squeezing it to make the sap flow
is like the cross. Every time you sin
you pound in another nail.
You make Jesus bleed. And his blood
is the only thing that quenches hellfire,
blots out sin. That's God's mercy.

This lesson is between you, me and Almighty God.

In the main my mortal sins consisted of
deliberate disobedience and impure thoughts.

Regarding deliberate disobedience,
admittedly I was an habitual sinner,
a bad little boy, and had been so for years,
though the enormity of my sin was a revelation.

But in my seven years and six months of life
I had not had even one impure thought,
until Granny explained, vaguely, where I ought not look,
nor touch, regarding myself or young ladies,
that this would lead to impure thoughts, adultery.
Within two days I lusted after Annie Dulciente,

with her sweet smile, deep brown eyes,
and shoulder length, shimmering black hair.
My sin was ever before me, beside me in class
and living just three doors away.

Father Vincent smelled of coffee,
Sir Walter Raleigh pipe tobacco,
my father's brand, and, occasionally, beer.
He had credited me with any number
of deliberately disobedient acts in the past,
but refused to believe I'd advanced to adultery.

We debated through the veil
in the confessional gloom
and settled on impure thoughts.

He granted absolution and gave me ten Hail Mary's.
I promised God I'd be good, sin no more,
cross my heart and hope to die
boil in oil and burn in fire. Amen

But Annie was on her front porch.
The wind played with her hair.
Her smile was sunshine.
She waved at me when I passed.

I had three impure thoughts
before I got home.

My father found me at the stove
building courage for the flame.

Grammy took off her glasses at dinner
between the stew and the pie,
spoke her mind while the coffee pot gurgled.

I'm moving to Florida.
To stay in this house

is to condone this house.
I'm leaving Thursday.

Dad handed her a slice of rhubarb pie,
Gee, Mum, we'll miss you.

I knew my father lied.
I knew lying was a sin.
But knew, just this once,
God didn't care.

First Grade Theology

"God's not really real, you know,"
Phillip jammed his maroon hat down
to his orange red eyebrows,
wound a long blue and white scarf
three times about his neck.

"Is so real," and we stepped out
from Hamilton Street Elementary,
two wool clad walking cocoons,
into five below for our trek home
on the Watertown, New York tundra.

"The grownups made it up.
They use him to keep kids in line."

We traded "is not" and "is to" along the siding,
trying to balance on the long sliver of cold steel
cleared of snow and ice by the freight train
trundling along in no hurry to pick up milk
from the Hygienic Dairy.

You could ride that train all the way
to New York City, if the hobos didn't get you.

Phillip slipped off the rail and
tumbled down the embankment
through snow and frozen pussy willows
to land on the creek that shared its bed
with the New York Central right of way.

"This stuff is frozen hard."
He jumped up and down until his hat fell off.
The ice cracked with a soft fierceness,
like distant thunder muttering under its breath.

Grey water pooled on top of the pale ice
as he scrambled up the bank.
"That was close," he panted.

"That was a warning.
Keep it up and God's gonna getcha."

"God's just made up."

"Yeah? Then go get your hat."

Phillip looked down at the wet maroon blotch
already freezing into the new glaze on the creek.
Then looked at his boots, from the ankles down
crusted in fresh ice. He rapped one foot against the rail.
Shards shattered, gleamed pink in the fading December light.

He told his mother a fifth grader swiped his hat.

In the Beginning

I was four, my brother almost seven
when I first went to the rail
on Ash Wednesday.

"Remember child, thou art dust,
and unto dust thou shalt return."

Back in the pew
I touched my gritty forehead.
"What'd he mean, 'Thou art dust.'?"

"It means you're gonna die."

I had not considered this possibility,
but, having attended my grandmother's funeral
and seen her incense wreathed casket
disappear into the ground just last month,
my brother's pronouncement
seemed appallingly plausible.

And, since he knew for certain
what I had not even suspected,
that I would die,
I sought further knowledge

and pointed at Saint Joseph
shrouded, halo to toe,
in opaque purple silk.

"How come he's all wrapped up?"

"That's not him. He's gone.
That's a ghost. They're all ghosts."

I looked around and found
purple specters everywhere,
on pedestals, on pillars,
lunging from wall niches.

Sunday I refused to dress for church
on the grounds I was not going.

After some discussion my father asked,
"Who told you they were ghosts?"

I knew then, my brother had lied.
Just as I knew, that if I told,
he would get a spectacular whipping.

Cain and Abel,
Jacob and Esau,

as it was in the beginning,
is now, and ever shall be.

I told.

Sister Victoria

With one soft word Sister Victoria,
youngest of Holy Family School's holy terrors,
culled me from the fourth grade homebound herd.
Her quiet steel voice clamped down on my heart
and snared my feet. Froze time.

The realization that she had used my first name,
Kenneth, naked, no "Young Mr." preface,
the relief that she held no ruler,
ready to whistle through the air in the holy name of God,
slowly reanimated the universe and my heart.

She glided from behind her desk,
centered herself in front of the slate board
spattered with sentences diagramed in yellow chalk.
Her pale hands framed by her dark habit
spread in a slow disembodied pirouette.

"Report to Father Mills for acolyte instruction.
Your close participation in the Mass will provide
the opportunity to discern if you have a vocation.
Christ has made priests out of young men no worse than you.
Do you know why you have been given this chance?"

Her brown eyebrows, the only hair I had ever seen on her,
or any nun, arched toward the starched triangle
of crisp white sailing her forehead, reinforcing the black robe
that proclaimed her a bride of Christ, dead to worldly snares.
Her green eyes glistened like stained glass at sunset.

"Because Phillip Thurston laughed.
Laughed, when Bishop Donatello stumbled.
Laughed at the foot of the very altar of God.
God has a special wrath for such a sin.
See to it that you never laugh. Never."

110 North Pleasant Street, 1955

Gram lived across the street
in a house of wonder with three goldfish,
calico, black and ruby, that circled eternally
about an undersea castled volcano
festooned with hydrilla and erupting
every ninety seconds in bubbles.

Their fantails danced in the water,
undulated and shimmied in the sun
like the lace window curtains
that quivered when her coal fired
furnace shook the air.

Bundick Colliers delivered a thunder load
of blue Pennsylvania anthracite monthly.
Every child on the block knew that truck's schedule,
assembled on delivery day under Gram's apple tree
to watch the chute stretch, touch her house,
hear the artillery roar of warmth delivered.

Only I was privileged to enter,
take the scuttle from the kitchen
descend into the cellar and return,
delivering a chalice of black heat for her stove,
receiving a slice of rhubarb pie for my effort,
eating it with Gram in the company of koi.

How the other children envied me.

The Making of Grandfather Frog
        For Thornton Burgess

Our parents drove out State Street
past the old ice plant,
it's crenulated cinderblock front
hiding a roof holed by time.
We came to where houses thinned
into pastures and orchards
and a limestone bridge crossed Cole Creek.

Parent parked in stone shade,
toes in water, bottom on the sand bank,
face bracketed between my knees,

I watched my brother and sister
chase down tadpoles,
penning them in mason jars.

I was too young to be trusted
in treacherous six inch deep current.

In the long shadowed twilight
Tom gathered sand and weed.
Sue picked over her candidates
to select the one ready for promotion.

Crammed between my siblings
I held the gallon jar on the ride
back to North Indiana Avenue,
one hand resting lightly over its mouth
to keep water from sloshing out.

Mom sang "Galway Bay"
and "I'll Take You Home Again, Kathleen"
in her soft church choir soprano.

Dad's bass rumbled the widows with
"The Cider Mill in Tiderville"
and "The Horse Named Napoleon".
The moon followed us home.

For weeks I dragged my lime green chair
to the kitchen counter to stare at our changeling,
squiggling slowly in pale tan water
where kosher pickles once slumbered,
growing legs while its body bulked,
its tail thinned and shrank to a stub.

I was again the honored guardian of the jar
when we drove to Westcott's Beach
to liberate our almost-frog,

celebrating his release with a day on the water,
a moated sandcastle with popsicle stick drawbridge,
an evening feast of hot dogs and corn on the cob.

A dream came to me
while I slept the way home;

our frog, grown big, seated on a lily pad,
smiling while the Merry Little Breezes laughed
and blew foolish green flies into his mouth.

Listening to Runa

Her back yard orchard of thorn apple, rhubarb
and raspberry bush, all free for the plucking,
fabled in the twilight starred with fireflies
rising from deep spectered shadows

where a pale Elfin Lord lurked in the gloom,
seeking summer's unwary boys
who prayed, but not often enough,
who failed to say their morning prayer,

foolishly believing last night's hurried
now-I-lay-me-down-to-sleep
extended protection beyond the bed,
won God's permanent affection.

Such prayers evaporate on waking,
need be renewed with a kneeled
Jesus-guide-me-through-my-day
to grant safety to any rising morrow.

The Earl of Dusk snatches these boys away
to entertain his soulless king at court
seated on his white throne of bones
stolen from the lost tomb of Solomon.

Under the Erlkönig's royal smile of sharp white teeth
careless, prayerless child captives in grey cloaks
twirl and spin across a flickering marble floor,
checkered in spite and malice, fire and ice.

They dance Mephisto's Waltz to the rhythm
of a kettle drum made of Goliath's skull,
a moaning flute shaped from his thigh bone,
the notes so low they make the walls quake.

The Elf King laughs while children cry silent tears
to keening violins strung with mermaid hair
stroked languidly with a bow fashioned from
a widow's dream, a drowned sailor's hope.

The younglings' tears give up little puffs of frost
when they strike sparkling fiery squares,
tiny puffs of flame on finding opalescent ice,
blossom into small sobs that keep time to the music.

After a night where hours eat decades
a raven lights on the Erlkönig's crown
to rasp of coming dawn. Freed, the dancers
stumble home under the last shadows,

young boys still. They find chimneys tumbled,
their names forgotten by feeble siblings
grown ancient, frightened of grey cloaked strangers,
their parents long laid beneath mossed stones.

Liquid silver faerie laughter
sings in their ears, mocks them
all the days of their lives,

follows them down to the grave
where they lie, children still,
while the world grows old.

Roads Taken

When trees and teachers were taller,
and the near woods deep,
I knew a place where the rocks spoke.

Two stone browed hills,
cliff faced, confronting,
of a height to bring a cold ache,
to freeze my feet, yet draw my head
and arc my whole frame till I can see,
just barely, past the edge.

The birch below
frame the twisting rills
till they braid into a clear stream
strained of leaf and mold
through sieve of dropped twig
brittled by frost, felled by wind.

I see, just barely, past the edge
to the birch below,
sharp as greenbrier.

They will impale me if I slip.

Yet from the north brow I hurl my soul
and hear three clear replies,
before the voices murmur into each other.

* * *

The elder children
who hunt these woods,
hunt me.

They are older and speak knowingly
of weapons, sheath knives and .22's,
they have hidden in the woods.

They are older and speak knowingly
with words they have taken from movies.
Movies I am not allowed to go to.

                * * *

There are many ways through these woods,
open paths, known to all.
I choose other paths.

Hidden paths that take me,
almost,
to where the rocks speak.

The last steps cross
a barren crown
of weathered granite.

Those who hunt these woods,
will see me.

Yet I must seek the edge
to hear my voice.

The Gravity of the Situation

On the last Tuesday before finals
Mr. Parker stood with his stopwatch
a safe distance from the point of impact
and, surrounded by his skeptical fourth grade,
gave the word. The janitor, Mr. Redstone,
everybody called him Red,
made the release out a third floor window
where the steep hillside dropped away.

The class witnessed the simultaneous impact
of three spherical pounds of steel
and one marble, a cat's eye shooter.

For an encore Red unspooled a reel of twine
until the end hovered above the dirt.
Peter was anointed to press it tight
while the janitor severed the cord
and let it flutter down.

The class marveled at how close Mr. Parker's numbers,
scribbled rapidly on the blackboard,
came to the feet and inches of string
Peter and his classmates had measured in the hall.

A discussion of Galileo, constant acceleration,
and how to measure seconds
with heartbeat or spoken word
finished out the day, air resistance
and terminal velocity left for fifth grade.

That summer Peter took his knowledge
into the nearby forest reservation.
With the drop of a pebble he discovered
the height of the cliff he threw hello off
to hear it repeated was eighty feet.

Later, he took Doreen Cheney to the cliff's edge
hoping to impress her with his echoes and learning.
When the stone dropped she kissed him.
The stone is dropping still.

Wakefield

One Saturday when I was nine,
I saw a man coming down the commons.
I had just thrown my morning papers
and was waiting for G. C. Murphy to open
so I could spend some of my tips
before reporting them to my mother.

As I Idled in the clear chilly sunlight
by the almost budding daffodils
sundialing the Minute Man statue,
he approached clad in a black bathrobe
and top hat, carrying an ebony cane,
its silver tip paling in the morning light
against dead white shins and bare feet.

He cut the air with his cane,
cursing, at someone who wasn't there,
swearing with words that were new to me,
"Infamous Bastard! Foul Miscreant!"

As he got louder, and nearer,
swinging, jabbing, stabbing the cane,
I realized several people were not there,
that he was the victim of a committee.

I edged along the daffodil clock
placing the bronze sentry
between myself and the bathrobed man,
keeping him six hours away,
watching him slice the air with cane and word.

I tracked him crossing the commons
coming to Lake Quannapowitt
and stopping, waist deep,
slashing the water with his cane.

"Leave me alone, or I'll kill us all!"

I slipped off the sundial to the police station.

Monday, on page three, a small article.
No names, just, "alert newspaper boy"
and, "returned to the safekeeping of Danvers State."

New Bedford

The houses stride, red brick, white pillared, down Union Street.
Captain Meredith's manse the center of a parade of wealth,
a full flight to the ivy pillared front porch, first of three stories.

The widow's walk, a glassed in crown, weather tight,
bristling with lightning rods, a tower of vigilance
thrust above its neighbors to spy on the bay, four miles south.

Rachel peers across the town, morning, noon, and evening,
a Congregationalist Angelus, searching the bay,
daughter Marie braced before her, awaiting their namesake,
the *Rachel Marie*, to bring home husband and father.

They have peered into glare and mist five years.
Marie is eight. She does not remember her father.
She remembers only his name. Only climbing stairs
and waiting for a man called Matthew.

> Their long stare saddens the town.
> They marvel at it in the barber shop.
> The bootblack repeats all he hears.

In the Portuguese quarter there is no maritime graveyard.
But the Irish of Saint Mary's raised a limestone obelisk
carved two years ago, lacking a date for none is known.

The names lost Catholics scrolled beneath an image of the ship,
Juan Da Villa, coopers mate, only son of the Azores aboard,
named third in a litany of drowned Irish whalers.

> The stone gave comfort to the quarter.
> They spoke of it in the fish market,
> women sorting scallops and solace.

The Congregational Church attempted a marker.
Rachel Meredith would not subscribe,
barred the carving of his name.

He is not lost. You have not proof nor right.
Subscriptions returned, marble uncarved,
while words cut and pew seats changed.

>	The cold quarrel divided the town.
>	They took sides in the barber shop.
>	The bootblack sped word of the squabble.

Captain Meredith had not owned quite half his ship,
but the first mate held two shares, the second another,
and the three men's controlling voice sailed as one.
At forty months out no returning whaler carried word.

None had sighted her since she slipped south of Nantucket,
Antarctic bound to water teeming with blue leviathan,
where gales stole ships and lives with grey indifference.
Rachel Marie, but one in a port home to more than eight score.

>	This did not then concern the town.
>	What little was said in the barber shop
>	the bootblack did not bother repeating.

The backers on shore dwelt in calm quiet anticipation.
The *Rachel Marie* carried little debt and much insurance.
Her return profitable, train oil high, spermaceti candles dear,
but loss would serve as well, that's what policies were for.

Money did not care how it was made, nor bankers.
They met with Rachel to present the hard fact,
to patiently talk sense, to make her a widow.
Shown the papers, Rachel Meredith demurred.

He will bring his ship to port. I will not sign.
The men from Hartford sided with Rachel and their wallet.
After festering in court, another year's interest earned,
another premium collected, the men from Hartford paid.

Rupert Russell, eldest backer and family friend,
he had courted Rachel's mother in his youth, paid a call
carrying the captain's share in hand. She served Assam tea,
the only warmth in the parlor that June morning.

The money is not mine. It would be theft to take it.
When Matthew returns, he will set things right.
Rupert left, went to the New Bedford Institute for Saving,
abandoned her portion there, and never thought on it again.

Captain Meredith had the forethought to insure his life as well.
When the agent came to pay Rachel for her husband,
she did not give him tea, but met him at the door,
called her driver to thrash him and throw him off the porch.

> This entertained the town.
> They laughed about in it the barber shop.
> The driver drank well on the tale.

No agent called on the Portuguese and Irish.
If only the courts had not taken so long to decide,
then the policies would still have force. A shame.

But in four and a half years of no husbands
money shrank. With premiums unpaid, policies lapsed.
Pity, that. The men from Harford did not pay on pity.

> Anger blew through the quarter.
> Men quarreled off loading cod,
> iron words landing with pollock.

Rachel's money short, her backers share grown
but untouched, her account dormant,
insurance rejected, she let the servants go.
Save the maid, who now must cook and sew as well as clean.

Save the driver, who now must tend the grounds,
repair the broken and lift the heavy.
Rachel and Marie learned to dress themselves,
to do their own laundry, iron their own clothes.

>   This was known to the town,
>   though not mentioned in the barber shop.
>   The bootblack already knew.

Maria Da Villa cooked for the Merediths ten years.
A decade of tasteless meals, little salt, less pepper,
boiled vegetables, the spices of her own hearth
and homeland forbidden to the table,
her livelihood ended with a fistful of coin.

Your services are no longer required.
You may keep the apron. Good day.
The shabby smallness of that gift absurd;
Rachel forgetting that Maria had bought the cloth
with her own copper, sewn it with her own hand.

In short weeks the widow Da Villa grew desperate.
Stiff rent and five children to feed, she stole:
a stale loaf, a spoilt sausage, and two withered onions.

To hide her shame, she robbed in the Irish market.
They did not know her need. She was caught, tried.
The court room rang for Mrs. Da Villa.

Neighbors pled for her. The priest defended her.
Her accuser spoke. If he had know Maria's plight,
he would have handed her twice what she took.
The judge was moved to pity

and gave out only thirty days.

> They muttered of riot in the quarter.
> Men dug at pavement. Stones flew,
> gifts for the bank from the fish market.

Rachel and Marie still climb to look out across the bay,
the habit of five years prodding their steps.
Rachel yet stares at empty water in hope.
Marie has begun to doubt.

> Their sorrow saddens the town.
> They still marvel in the barber shop,
> but the bootblack no longer cares.

Mrs. Da Villa's durance ends tomorrow.
Father Rentoa has taken up a collection.

> There is sullen anger in the quarter,
> women and men with tight grey faces,
> but her children dance in the fish market.

August in the Berkshires

I am too long a dweller of the country
to tolerate the trucks of Great Barrington.
They gear down on US 7, dropping into town,
grumbling to a stop at the lights
that populate the Barrington Cañon,
three blocks long, three stories tall.

The brick and glass amplification of traffic
drives me into Yellow House Books.
I burrow deep into the insulation
of General Fiction, World Wars One & Two,
Juvenile Series and Regional Interest.
The third room in offers Poetry, Plays and silence.

Reinforced with Marlowe and Heaney,
fortified on my way by the SoCo Creamery's
coffee ice cream, I return to my hills,
to the quieter roar of a summer night,
the gentle savage pulse of katydids,
the occasion boom of Grandfather Frog
from his still pond, laughing at the moon.

Chipmunk and Granite

Does the chipmunk know
that its world of stacked pink and grey granite,
shattered boulders the size of doghouses
for Great Danes down to mere Chihuahuas,
holds back the dunes and land,
keeps my house from sliding into the bay?
No. No, he does not.

But the chipmunk does know
death floats on the clear air
coming in from the sea
rising up over the dunes.

Knows a red-shouldered hawk
straddles this rail of wind
rolling a wing every now and then,
shifting its tail to cup more air
when the sea breeze softens,
beak and eye steady
as if he were perched on stone,
on the very granite the chipmunk
peers out from under.
This, the chipmunk knows beyond all else.

The Old Men of the Sea

Seals are the old men of the sea,
lolling on their backs, arms crossed,
chest awash with the sun.
Waves rippling under grey whiskered faces
gently lift elder heads,
chuck them under the chin
then glide away toward the reeds
surrounding Little Spaniel Island
put out of reach by the falling tide
and a narrow steeply sloped strip of sand.

They slumber on their backs
in the golden warm shallows,
safe from the great white sharks
that hunger in the black depths
that lie on the other side of the drying bar.

Soon the moon will change her mind,
put her shoulder to the sea,
lift salt wave over the strand,
batter at the seal gate
until full three fathoms
of dark murk hide the shark
as he slithers in to hunt.

The old men of the sea will feel the chill,
sense the currents and move on,
long before their foe crosses over.

It's how they got to be old.

Man with a Blown Guitar

The man with a Blown Guitar
sits on the concrete bench
in front of the Provincetown Hall
and plays with reckless oblivion
to such niceties as rhythm, melody,

or even his B string,
a casualty of his
determined assault
on "Lay, Lady Lay".

It twists in the air, one parted strand
grasping at his fretting hand,
the other tangling his staccato beat
into a flamenco waltz.

An almost young golden tan man,
to whom wrinkles will come later,
when the sun has had time
to teach him tan means leather,

for now his open shirt
displays curly sunlight
covering a broad chest.
A modest Budweiser tumor

bulges against his guitar.
His cut offs are uneven,
one thigh high,
one knee low.

His discordant performance
could be forgiven, were he drunk.
I pass close enough to share his air.
He is not drunk, not yet.

Though he clearly was last night,
and, just as clearly, has not bathed since,
but has had breakfast. Traces of
over easy eggs speckle his beard.

His battered Stetson clone
holds only a seed dollar.
If I toss in some money
will he stop to thank me?

How much am I prepared to pay
for quiet? How big a bribe?
Would a twenty pack him off,
or just encourage him?

And if this is going to be about money,
how shall we auction off the morning?
Who would place their bid for music?
Who, but me, would bid the morning be silent?

Coffee, After Labor Day

I find the traffic light enough driving
along the Grand Army of the Republic.
But here on Minister's Pond
it pierces the tree breeze
to shatter the morning
with the sound of small car fire.

Two southbound truckers letting off the gas
for the Eastham stop light
give out the dull rapid thud-bark
of a pair of fifty cals,
spaced at two hundred meters,
interlocking their field of fire.

The grey catbird patrols her stand
of pitch pine, locust and white oak,
passes by the black cherry
set with its bitter fall fruit,
to rest in the solitary white birch
to the left of the little beach
of truck delivered yellow sand.
Her hoarse cry protests my intrusion
or the traffic. I'm not sure which.

The ring my coffee cup makes
when I press it into the coarse grains
will disappear in the next rain.

Old Men of Chatham

The old men of Chatham
ply their craft in vessels
that set out upon the sea
two hours before dawn
to slay dogfish, spiny and smooth.

Loading down small boats
with their livelihood,
they return at mid-day
to find monk seals in the harbor
waiting to be fed at the docks.

Safe here from the great white
that lunges up from deep waters,
they dine on the scraps
of the white's distant, lesser cousins.

The offspring of Chatham
work beside their elders
slowly trading their tans for leather,
becoming, but not yet, old.

It is they who toss the offal,
grin at squabbling gulls,
seals exploding from below
to end the dispute.

They are yet young.
Death still amuses them.

Used Book Store

Danger! Keep Out!
Unprocessed Books

The sign forbad entry into a cluttered room.
I paused to digest the warning,
evaluate the risk.

Were unprocessed books
the same as uninoculated books?
Were they occasionally rabid?
If one nipped me on the ankle,
would I have to get shots?
The big needle, right in the stomach?

Or were the dangers post consumption?
What were the consequences
of undercooked prose?
of ingesting raw poetry?
unsafe thoughts?
Did I even want to know?

I decided to risk it,
and emerged, unnoticed,
with M. R. James'
A Warning to the Curious.

The store I visited was I Cannot Live Without Books, 314 Main St. (Route 28), West Dennis, MA 02670.

Cape Cod Cats

Low water at dawn at the edge
of the high tide's grasp,
searching past the sand flats
to where catboats sail away.

I savor the sea on sharp breeze blunted
and turned by beard and pea coat.
Wet smells of mud and mollusk,
the scent of life, flow through me.

The insistent wind drags scraps of fog
against the steep rock strewn hill,
gathering fleece in a flock at the base
against the coming sun, a daily futility.

From the firmament
over the tawny gold marsh
the narrow pier of salt-silvered wood reaches out
to catch the running wave,
hold back the fleeing tide.

Wheeling, keening, soaring,
tacking against the river of air
the gulls chase the catboats,
harry them past pine-studded
Strong Island Marsh
to the cut in Chatham Bar,
where the Cape Cod cats sail free.

**Poem
of
Two Voices**

My father's staff made of saguaro gnarled, weathered and grey.	My mother's staff made of saguaro almost never noticed.
My father's staff bound in nylon cord tied off in a Jesus-knot.	My mother's staff bound in nylon cord tied off in a Jesus-knot.
My father's staff lean and limber, bent, almost cracked.	My mother's staff lean and limber, bent, almost cracked.
My father's staff leans against the wall beside my mother's staff.	My mother's staff leans against the wall beside my father's staff.

They lean,
one against the other.

If the wall fell,
they would stand.

Good Is Not Interred

Standing behind a dark oak podium,
drawing the deep breath of fortitude,
preparing to sum up to a full chapel,
and all of Tucson that cared to hear,
my father's life and worth,
when a man stepped inside the church.

Late, he hurried down the aisle.
I paused. Gave him time to find a seat.
Straight to the communion rail,
he knelt and crossed himself three times.

Skinny, five foot six, dark,
deeply tanned, high cheekbones,
his face leathered and lined
by the actinic Arizona sun,
somewhere between fifty and seventy,
well scrubbed, a ragged haircut
with two cowlicks, three days of beard,
and dressed in a once bright plaid suit coat,
worn, sun faded, clearly the best thing he owned,
in a quiet strong voice he called my father by name,

thanked Dad for everything he had done,
deeds we knew nothing of.
He rose, genuflected and,
with another triple sign of the cross, left,
went back to whatever the homeless
called home, where ever that was in Tucson.

Comb

My mother's gift of two pair of pants,
grey wool, worn only to church
by my father, which was often,

his favorite socks, an electric blue
even his colorblind eye could see,

and, oddly, his comb,
long and narrow, tapering,
wide teeth to fine,

grief wandering the path of generosity,
pain throwing out lifelines
to children and any passerby.

In time the pants grew tight.
They go to church now
on someone else's legs.

In time the socks grew holes
beyond memory's repair
and I discarded them.

I still use the comb
when I wet my hair in the morning
and set it right for the day,

raking a careful part and casual wave,
then running it once through my beard,
just as my father did.

Its teeth are decades brittle,
a few are missing.

Some things won't let go.

Temporary Repair

Window on the back wall of this garage
has nine panes, three tall and three wide,
eight of dust webbed glass,
too far back from the work bench to clean.

That's what Dad told Mom,
don't know that she believed him
but she let it go in time.
And one wooden pane, dead center.

Glass blew out in sixty-four.
Nor'easter took it. Didn't touch the house.
Not a shingle out of place, roof nor siding.
But it turned one garage pane to slivers and grit.

Dad pawed through odd pieces of wood
for a shingle that was just-right-too-big,
laid it on his bench. Used a piece of angle iron
for a straight edge and scored it with a box cutter.

He hummed "Feller from Fortune" under his breath
while he worked the score over and deeper
till the trim fell off and left a perfect fit.
Did it all by eye.

It looked odd the first year,
cedar gold centered
in grey grimed glass,
but it salt silvered soon enough.

Kept the rain out fine,
and the wind mostly.
It whispered in the breeze,
hummed in a strong wind,
get to moaning in a full gale.

Fill the house for days,
come a winter nor'easter.

"Sailors lost at sea," Dad said.

"Lost souls in purgatory,
begging to be let out," Mom said.

Lasted forty-five years,
twelve more than Dad did.
Thunderstorm popped it out Memorial Day.
Didn't break it. Just spit it on the floor
and slid it under Mom's Hyundai.

Didn't touch anything else,
window, tree or shingle,
just Dad's pane. Spite, I guess.

I saw where he went wrong, shakes taper,
and Dad's chosen shingle was no exception.
The lower edge shifted in the wind,
let in the whistle. Back and forth, all those years,
all that moving, all that time, bound to break free.

I cut two narrow strips of duct tape,
grey, to match the wood,
and built the lower edge up
to make a wind proof fit.

Called up Mom after the next storm
to find out how she and the wood pane
weathered. "Don't know. The hum's gone.

In the twelve years since I buried your father,
every storm, I heard him out there,
working at his bench, humming to himself,
and now he's gone. Gone all over again."

So I'm back in the garage,
peeling grey tape
from a grey shingle,
reinstating my father's mistake.

You can't argue with time.

The Geography of Leaves

A time of leave taking,
a time of letting loose
the fastening that bind us
to our particular reality,
a time of falling from our trees
into separate geographies.

The idea of separation
and growth
has been stressed and pressed
beyond recognition.

A flimsy construction,
at best
an apology for necessity,
it blinds us
with insidious familiarity,

forbids us our protest
and leaves us mumbling
promises of return.

In Memoriam

I cram myself into the passenger seat
of my wife's silver Civic, reach down,
throw the lever and slide myself back
unkinking my knees,

just as my wife reaches down,
throws the lever and slides herself up
to reach the pedals.

Our seats were opposite to our custom
Last time out I drove,
chauffeuring our company,
freeing my wife for conversation.

To ease our too tall son-in-law's legs,
Carolyn pulled her seat forward.
Just as I slid mine back,
knowing our too short daughter
could spare the room.

And they remained like that,
off kilter, silent memorials
to our last excursion
before our guests returned to Florida.

Now we casually shift them again
and impress a new memorial
on our private world,
overwriting the old,

a monument to the way thing are,
now that the children are gone.

Visiting Doris

Aunt Doris had a color television in the living room,
where we watched cartoons
and wrestling on rainy Saturdays.
She made me popcorn with sinful amounts of butter
for Sunday night Disneyland.

Doris kept a black and white TV in her basement
where she provided a running commentary
on "The Guiding Light" and sipped Crème d'Abricot
from a tiny hourglass shaped bottle
while I folded sheets, hot from her dryer.

Once we walked six blocks downtown
to The Golden Sugar Bowl
where she bought two hot fudge sundaes,
tipping the waitress a dollar
for seventy cents worth of ice cream.

The Sugar Bowl, long torn down.
Doris's home, The Parkview Bed & Breakfast,
run by a young couple from Boston.
Yet she waves to me from the porch
every time I drive by.

Magna Cum Latte

My brother, lured to live in Los Angeles
by an agent unencumbered by ethics,
called me from the set
between takes twelve and thirteen.

"Used to jog across Central Park,
wave to the dog walkers,
slam a bagel and latte from the deli,
lope back, shower and hit the casting calls.

Can't walk in L. A. Gotta hava car.
Nearest decent bodega,
twenty minutes of kamikaze traffic.
I'm givin' up. Gonna buy a coffee pot."

A desperate move for an actor
who has never brewed,
always bought, his coffee.

He will master this skill
like a character in a scene,
shaping stage directions and bare lines,

into Cunningham, the recruiter,
courting Joaquin, the priest's younger brother,
with sly admiration and shared confidences,

slowly leading him toward the necessary signature,
stymied only when the script sends him home
robbing my brother of his prey,
saving Joaquin for a smaller, more dangerous, war.

He will build his cup of coffee
the way he built Sgt. Cunningham,
with patience and endless rehearsal,

bean or ground? Columbian or Honduran?
cream, whole milk or two percent?

Crafting the perfect cup, holding the perfect latte,
and with it, the crisp morning air of Central Park,
as yet unfouled by traffic, a toasted sesame bagel,
mellowed by honey butter, and the cheerful voice
of the man at the register who calls all his regulars by name.

Parades
(For Laurel Massé)

She was an almost lost little child
dancing in the gap between formations,
fifteen feet behind her daddy,
who had just won World War II
and should be leading this parade.

Strutting proudly in front of the Watertown
Fire Department Fife and Pipe Band,
black hair, red ribbons, royal blue jumper,
waving her drum major's baton,
a willow wand cut from the backyard.

She kept perfect time as she a sang scat solo
lost under the drone of the highlands,
but loud enough and strong enough
to glow in her mind for decades.

Seventy-five now with a walker,
a cane on her good days,
and this is one of them.

The fire truck sirens wail,
the syncopated drums pound,
quicken her rheumatic heart,
and the pipes, oh how they call.

But she can't push through
to join the march and sing,
to mark her time, beating the air
with an orthopedic baton.

The crowd will not part
for the little girl with a cane,
in her dowdy black dress,
her sensible black shoes,

her grey hair tied back
in a bun with a satin ribbon,
red, shiny as the 4th of July.

Sirens

We were in a borrowed Carolina Skiff
approaching the Cape Charles harbor,
Peter forward, holding down the bow,
myself in the stern, hand on the throttle,
wrapped in a cocoon of outboard rumble,
thinking of Jason and his Argonauts,
the geography of the Golden Fleece.

I had puzzled over this as a boy.
The librarian assisted me in dragging
an oversized historical atlas
to the great polished mahogany table.

Jason clearly went through the Dardanelles
and over the Black Sea to Colchis
hard against the Georgian coast.

He took a different route back and ended up in Crete.
I couldn't work that out.
There was no other way out of the Black Sea,
just the Dardanelles or the Dardanelles.

And you can't sail on land,
even if you are Jason son of Aeson,
rightful king of Thessaly, with a witch queen
and the Golden Fleece onboard.

Peter bellowed through the sound wall,
"Sirens!" And pointed into the wind.

I wanted to shout, "Don't listen to them!
They sing from the jetty promising joy eternal
if you'll just dive in and come to their side.
You'll never reach them. Water and granite
will compete for your destruction.
It will not matter who is the victor.

The last sound you will hear,
when the mocking laughter fades,
will be the eldest siren saying,
'Let us find another.'
If you would live, stop up your ears."

Instead I followed his arm across the slips
to Mason Street and saw, not Odysseus,
writhing in a Tantalus of lust,
tied to his mast while deaf oarsmen
rowed oblivious through deadly melody,
but only the Cape Charles Fire Department
taming a minor conflagration.

I throttled down and glided to our mooring,
killed the engine and watched silently
while Pete snugged the bowline
of our Argo to a horn cleat.

I shouldered my oar
and stepped ashore knowing
that no one will wonder
at my length of wood
or why I wander,
myth to myth.

Fedoras

The wrinkled old man in the light blue shirt
with red suspenders sits at the sidewalk table
in front of the Cape Charles Coffee House
and glances over his paper from under his fedora.

Not one of the jaunty hats of today
sold in an assortment of tweed and green,
twill and herringbone. Not the kind I wear,
a youthful hat to set off my white beard.

Rather, my father's hat,
the kind worn in the days
before we numbered wars.

The kind you see in old news reels,
the overhead shot of Main Street,
an angry sea of fedoras marching
to the recruiter's office on December 8th
without one whitecap of naked hair.

The scene did not have to be shot in color
for you to know that every hat was grey.

Waiting for Fish

Fragments of words shimmy on the wind
rip across the Cape Charles Fishing Pier,
mingled with the mumbling of cranes
shifting concrete across the harbor

and the clatter of rip rap
backhoeing its way
from railcar to barge
by the harbor master's shed.

Walking toward the summer fishermen
bait bucket and pole in hand,
I hear only syllables ripped from words
and jammed together, haphazard,

yielding no content, offering only tone,
leaving me ignorant of fish preferences,
squid or clam, biting or not,
but well aware the day is mellow,

as is the small knot of men
where the salt wood ends,
poles out over the water,
waiting for fish, or Godot.

Calico and Gold

The old lady next door
had eleven cats.

They sat in rows,
calico and gold, black and white,
like Van Gogh flowers,
gathering the sun on her back roof,

and made shady nests in the carpet of last year's leaves
that spread across the old lady's backyard like a lawn.

They came to her for food and conversation.
They came to me for food, but never said anything.

I watched them prowl my newly stacked firewood
with the graceful awkwardness
of a cat whose curiosity
has overcome caution and balance.

Looked out my kitchen window
while they roamed the neighborhood
and wondered how they got on her back roof.

I never saw them climb.
No Jacob's ladder
of cats ascending
and descending.

They were either
on her roof
or not.

She talked to them,
called them by name.
Called them by the names of old friends

who were careless enough to die
and leave her lonely.

I used to think she was crazy.
But now I have cats
and people tell me
I am getting old.

On the Superiority of Cats

We bury what dogs roll in.
If that is not sufficient proof,
you are probably a dog,
or an idiot. A distinction
without a difference.

The Advantages of Owning
A Magician

It's not all anchovies and cream,
owning a magician.

I'm lying low on the window sill
watching the yard under a sliver of moon.

Does the mouse see the owl
crouched on the silver pine branch?

I'll never know.

For when he enters the room
he must flip the switch.
I know he's night blind, but I'm not.

Nor are the owl and mouse,
and they're gone with the light,
taking my entertainment with them.

He's handy on a chill night,
warm lap and warmer bed,
and consistently provides fresh kill,
apparently without even hunting.

If that was the sum of his talent,
I'd consider replacing him.
But he has kidnapped a child of the sun
and keeps it captive in a metal cage.

This involved the admission of strangers
into the sanctuary, three humans,
two of which stank of dog.

He closed off the room for the installation,
but the stench was everywhere.

I think he's nose deaf as well night blind.

When the intruders left, I inspected the damage.
A black metal box sprouting a pillar to the ceiling
sat in the corner obstructing my favorite view.

It featured a window that revealed
a pile of large and small branches
and wadded rattle paper.

A thing unknown to me,
windows that looked in.

I was still considering the import
of this revelation,
when he opened the box,
muttered an incantation,
made a pass and, behold,
a sunling appeared.

Now on chill mornings,
after he has served me my milk and kill
and I have eaten as much as I care to,

I go to the sunbox and stare at it,
pointedly.

Then I stare at my magician,
pointedly.

He's fairly bright and gets right to it.
Feeds the sun beast wood,
large quantities of it.

Hard to credit, but,
I am telling you the truth;
sunlings eat wood, prodigiously.

Properly fed and prodded the sunling
toasts a rainy winter's day
and makes sleep a joy.

For this reason,
I keep my magician.

Although, come summer,
I may reconsider
the terms of his employment.

Carpe Diem Redux

She pointed out that the lawn urgently wanted mowing,
adding, "There is no time like the present."
I well knew that there was no time *but* the present.
Wisdom gained from a long marriage precluded my reply.

Gutters needed cleaning, the garage sweeping,
and the beginnings of a bird nest had appeared yesterday,
decorating the shelf above my workbench.
I'd hear no mention of this over the rumble of the mower.

Later, Heaney's *Beowulf* dragged me to my hammock
with a clear conscience and a jug of lemonade.

Seize the shade.

Wild Violets

Learn to love
   the wild violets.

They neither reap nor sow,
   nor need to.
Let them take the lawn
   if they will.

They are more pleasing to the bare foot
   than indifferently sprouted seed
   purchased and strewn with blind intent.

Your dog will roll in them
   and suffer only joy.

You can learn a lot
   from your dog.

Buddy Knows His Business

When he's taking his folk for a walk
and hears my little Ranger
puttering out my drive
Buddy steps to the shoulder.

After I come to a full stop
he ambles to the driver's side
and accepts his due,
two biscuits, one at a time.
Sometimes a third, maybe,
but the guarantee is two.

If Buddy has strolled on
past the corner into the field,
on hearing my truck
he'll pivot, catch my eye,
and drag his people back.

He knows I'll wait for him
just as he waits for me.
We have a ritual to consummate,
a deal to seal, with two biscuits,
sometimes three.

Hungars Creek Winter Time Blues

We never see blue jays but in winter and fall.
They drift into our yard in twos and threes,
bully the sparrow and finch for fun and spite,
disabuse the cardinal of his sunflower seed monopoly
and clear the feeder with a counterfeit hawk *scree*.
Bird and squirrel panic scurry away,
all but the flicker, too stupid to care
or too wise to be deceived, he stands fast.

As the days shorten and grey
two and three grow to six and eight.
Flashing squadrons, blue chevroned in white,
flit from feeder to ground snatching black seed
labeled "Oil rich for year-round birds".
The guarantee confirmed by a bright red cardinal
and pale purple house finch bracketing the printed word,
proof of their endorsement darting about our yard.

The jay's confident racket makes our cats
utter plaintive jaw quivering chitters
and press against the chill window
in frustrated predatory lust,
teased and inflamed by the jays' abrupt flight
as they flit up to the low braches of our alder
and shatter their prize against a bark anvil,
littering the ground with sunflower seed husks
like a Little League dugout after a game.

The heavy frosts and light snows of early December
draw raucous blackbird flocks to pepper our salt white yard.
They do not know our moves and flee every noise and shadow
while the jay ornaments our alder, patient puffballs of blue.
They have learned that shadow and sound prelude fresh seed

and flutter down to grab and hammer open their prize
before we have climbed the back steps to our porch.
One heavy snowfall I counted, twice for surety,
forty patient indigo splashes on stark snow laden limbs.

It minded me of when I was twelve in upstate New York
collecting on my paper route on Thursday nights
in brittle subzero cold. All the living room Christmas trees
with their early sixties red, white, blue, green and orange lights,
glowed up and down Bowers Ave and Haley Street.
But over on Ward, in the house I saved for last,
a bay windowed white flocked tree lit by a clear spot light
hung with hundreds of metallic blue glass ornaments
each topped with a frosting of glazed snow.

In March our ornaments start to dwindle.
By fooles' day they are few, by mid April none.
Now, in the second half of June, my wife remarks
on the brief return of one and its abrupt departure.
I have spread sunflower bounty and waited
for three days, much to the cardinal's delight,
but bringing me to the threshold of frustration
when, finally, the jay again graces our yard
and bangs a black oil seed open on a pine stump,
the solitary return of the winter time blues.

Hungars Creek Spring

1
Early Good Saturday, cleaning the churchyard,
chill air working in and out my lungs,
earnestly scraping leaves from the markers,
carved marble and granite, rich folk, even in death.
Raking a flurry of debris into the tarp,
Tom mentions a humming bird in his garden, just yesterday.

2
Easter Monday I stop my pickup for a box turtle.
Small, hurrying as much as a turtle can,
he (or she, hard to tell with turtles, boxed or no)
he is short of the safety of the woods by three feet.
I spot Zak's Ford and flag him down
pointing at the turtle, frozen now in caution.
We wait while she (or he, it's tough to tell)
recovers her courage and gains the woods.
Satisfied in a well invested ten minutes
we nod and go our ways.

3
Back home our lone laughing gull
no longer mocks her name with solitary keening.
There is a low tide with mud flats peeking through,
sun to warm the shallows,
fetch killifish from out the marsh reeds
and stir a circus of careening gulls
to a carousel of chaos and casual discord.

4
The black racer almost caught the skink
but fell back from the siding,
his prey now hanging from the gutter,
orange head swiveling in suspicion,
safe, but considerably more alert.
I advise the predator

"You're good for now,
but let Carolyn see you
and there'll be trouble."
The snake ignores me,
his eye on another skink.

5
Before the dawn wakes, we hear him,
down the slope by the marsh, over and over.
"Chuck willow, where you been so long?"
I murmur and slip back into sleep.

The Voice of the Turtle Is Heard in Our Land
Song of Solomon 2:12

We compost, but not watermelon rind.
That tidbit we set at the edge of our woods
leaving a glint of red for the night feeders,
raccoons, possums and such.

The inevitable does not wait on anticipation,
is indifferent to our surprise,
and we were surprised at our back porch lunch
when a box turtle showed up and made her own

off yesterday's melon.
Climbed all over it.
Thoroughly enjoyed the stuff.
Came back later for more.

Worked out well, we ate watermelon every day,
Carolyn, my wife, me and *Chompaire le Fem du Boxaire,*
(That's French, or ought to be.)
the name, a tribute to our turtle's appetite and gender.

A week later, two turtles, both boxed.
The new arrival we named, *Companyon,*
or, more formally, *Companyon de Chompaire.*
(Also French. Trust me on this.)

They got on well, *Chompaire* and *Companyon,*
until the tomato slice incident.
Turtles, it would seem, do not share well,
not when there is only one slice of tomato.

The dispute began poorly and did not improve,
sharp possessive nips at the crimson prize,
arched necks, hard hissings exchanged,
a brief, bitter tug-of-war.

Companyon marched off head high
making good speed. The ragged red remnant
a parasol of victory shading his way.
Chompaire wept into her melon.

I did not see this, the weeping.
Carolyn had the binoculars.
I can vouch for melancholy,
a subdued manner to her dining.

Her departure in a separate direction troubled us.
Carolyn had her opinions about *Companyon's* conduct.
I had reservations myself, but said nothing.
Rather, I went out and picked tomatoes.

The next day, they ate in peace,
A rind of melon, a slice of tomato, each.
Carolyn noticed sharp, sidelong glances from *Chompaire*.
I can't vouch for this. She had the binoculars.

Life went well.
Plenty of watermelon.
The tomatoes continued to ripen.
We shared our bounty.

Then came the third turtle,
Huzzie le Shammles,
(French, as you may guess.)
and she was not coy.

She strode out of the wood, bold, brazen,
sauntered between *Chompaire* and *Companyon*,
confident in the sway of her carapace,
she did not bother to glance back.

I did not need binoculars
to know that she was the Mae West of box turtles.

Nor did *Companyon*, who made lecherous pursuit,
toot sweet. (French, it's so expressive.)

For three days tomato and melon
went untouched by turtle lips.
Carolyn fretted, staring out the window.
I pretended to a stoic indifference.

On the fourth day, the return of *Chompaire, solitaire*.
She ate well, all the tomatoes and half her melon,
but displayed an air of melancholic wisdom.
I could tell. I had the binoculars.

Machipongo Mountain Range

Driving off Wilsonia Neck
into what should be the morning sun
I spy the Machipongo Range
across a mile and a half
of Del Monte staked tomatoes.

It rises beyond the tree lined field
perfect in its rumpled purple majesty
as the best of the Rockies
rising sharply out of the Colorado high plains
to greet the west bound motorists of I-70.

The Machipongo Mountains
advance rapidly with the speed
of the Atlantic squall that birthed them,
a little early in the season, and stronger for it.

Lightning cleaves the roiling boulders
and the avalanche rumbles down,
a moving talus slope of slate grey rain.

Machipongo Mists

Machipongo, from the Algonquin
for dusty place or sere land,
wraps itself in autumn mist
when the chill East Wind
corrals the Gulf Stream's humid breath
and herds it landward,
turns the air grey with water
that roils, twists, but does not fall.

The dirt road I walk on
raises corn yellow clouds
when my distant feet,
almost lost in the Atlantic haze,
break the thin film of dew
to free the dust below.

When the West Wind arrives from the bay
he will chivy the fog back out to sea
with hard rain or soft sun.
He does not yet wear fall's grey cloak.
Not till then will he bring me silver air.

The Old Man of Wachapreague

He doesn't travel fast. He doesn't travel far.
At ninety-three time tangles his feet.

Walking the warm nights of Wachapreague
he ends up on the bench at the foot of the dock.
The street light stretches that far and stops,
hiding the warped boards that lead to the boats
and trip old men in the dark.

He fills his pipe with Borkum Riff Bourbon Blend.
All his doctors forbid it.
All his doctors are dead.
The thought gives as much satisfaction
as the moist tobacco and soft smoke.

He's waiting for a summer tourist
restless in a small town offering only one bar
and a Little League game for night life.

Someone who needs to know
presidents and Rockefellers stayed here.
Wachapreague Hotel, built in oh two,
burnt down in seventy-eight,
used to stand right over there.

Came for the flounder. Fished all day.
Sinned all night. Little Sin City by the Sea.

Time tangles his feet,
not his memories.

At ninety-three
he remembers how good,
sometimes twice as good,
things used to be.

Tangier Island

The December Chesapeake
breathes its still warm humid breath
into the clear Tangier night sky

of gelid stars, bright on black
unhindered by the mercury lights
strung over Crisfield's streets

mocking with false full moons
what Tangier cloaks
in modesty and mystery.

From the dark bay's breath
comes an unfallen snow,
a blaze of salt white frost

that, flared red by the rising day,
will swiftly run through gold to silver,
into clear dew under the living sun.

The Company of Cats

He never married,
but walked all his days
in the company of cats,
tuxedos mostly, some greys,
a marmalade or two.

He urged patience
while dribbling milk into bowls,
coming to the door during storms
to let in a squall of cats.

He gave and asked their advice,
kept a constant flow of conversation.
No one on the island thought him odd.

He jes diffrent, s'all.
Always been diffrent.
Probbly always will be.

Toward the end the cats grew into
a following kaleidoscope of fur
ruled over by a calico and ginger
that waited for him on his neighbor's porch
when he went over to borrow a cup-of.

Like many who die on Tangier,
he is buried in his front yard.
Calico and ginger keep vigil,
rainy days from the porch,
sunny, purring through their naps
sprawled across his grassy chest.

Coffee at the Machipongo Trading Company

The old man moved my coffee out of the way,
crooked his left arm across the table
waved his right hand over his bicep
preparing a map of tan wrinkles.

This here's Hungars Creek. Goes on a bit.
He made a pass over his forearm.
Jacobus Creek, what I'm talkin' about.

Palm flat on the table he spread his fingers,
ring and little pressed together, veering off
from the other two, pressed together and holding fast.
He poked at the thumb stabbing back toward his chest.

Hickory Cove. Knuckle wrinkle's my house.
He moved up the prong of paired fingers.
South Branch. North Branch.
Back of my hand's the wide water.
Half a mile across at high tide,
more if the moon's pulling strong.

This time a the year the Canada geese,
the year-rounds, gather up.
Don't go anywhere, just fly the fields.
Winter-overs join 'em. Flock gets bigger.

Come evening there's a cloud of 'em,
thousand strong, bathed in sunset,
honking high hallelujahs all the way home,
spiraling in over the wide water.

Center of the flock drops down
like yarn from the wife's knittin' funnel.
One lands, swims away to the marsh
making room for another.

*It's a backwards tornado,
setting geese down
instead of picking 'em up.*

It's why I live here.

A Question I Have Pondered
Now and Again

How happy is a clam?
And what does it say about us
that this expression is in our language,
has, in fact, become a cliché?

I have never desired to be that happy.
This may be because I haven't a clue
how happy a clam is, and don't know anybody
who has a clue either.

Maybe I'm being too picky.
Maybe I'm missing something,
something everybody else knows.
Maybe I'm just being stupid, again.

I've done it before. In public. Like the time
they introduced me to the band, and I asked,
*If you guys are The Doobie Brothers,
how come nobody's named Doobie?*

When I shared my concerns, and confession of stupidity,
over an open mic to a late and somewhat thinned crowd,
a man with a red beard informed me in the tone
that comes from certain and absolute knowledge,

and a variable but large quantity of beer,
Clams are only happy at high tide.
No doubt my face betrayed my skepticism.
From the sound board Peg assured me this was true.

I looked about for confirmation.
The wait staff nodded in harmonious unison.
And what better place to receive this intelligence
than the Great Machipongo Clam Shack?

Still, I mulled the matter on the drive home
and pulled into my garage resolved to ask Tim,
my across the street neighbor, for confirmation.
He is a waterman and supplier of clams to the shack.

In the somber caffeinated morning
I thought more deeply on the issue.
Could Tim be trusted on this?
With my money and my life, absolutely.

But could a waterman be truly unbiased?
Was he not, and I do not mean to be pejorative,
a predator of shellfish, most especially clams?
Would it even be fair to put the question?

Does the coyote care about the rabbit?
Or the lion feel empathy with the antelope?
How could they survive if they did?
It's probable he has never considered the issue.

And would any answer he gave
alleviate my original concern;
is clam bliss so admirable,
that we should aspire to it?

The clam lives in mud, with luck, sand,
and is purported, twice a day, to be as happy as itself.
High tide is a brief moment, barely a pause,
before the water turns about face

and starts marching toward low tide,
constantly sloshing between two brothers
bitterly estranged since forever,
or at least the birthing of the moon.

Fraternal twins ever squabbling, over what?
The fleeting happiness of clams?
And if this proverb states our collective ambition,
how is it that we fail, so often, to clear so low a bar?

All Day

"So, how long have you been writing?"

I rolled my answer around my tongue:

At eighteen Professor Namir called one of my poems good.
In my early twenties I improved, got published on occasion,
paid fifty dollars once, half a month's rent back then.

In my mid twenties,
drinking began to interfere with writing.
In my late twenties,
writing began to interfere with drinking.
I knew I had to make a decision.

Two decades later I changed my mind,
stopped drinking. Nothing. Nada.
Not even beer.

But I saw he wanted the short answer,
so I said, "All day."

The Burden of Fame

There was a woman from the News
prowling the Clam Shack at the open mic,
pocket notebook in hand
asking questions,
writing down answers.
In time, she got around to him.

The man with the long lensed camera
got around to him too.

Eventually, they got around to everyone.
So he didn't think much about it.

Oh, he checked the paper Saturday.
Finding nothing, the matter slid from his mind,
leaving a trail of mild disappointment
as it wove its way down and out.

He really did forget about it.
And really was surprised Wednesday,
his name on page one,
picture on page three.

There were other names,
other photos.

But,
name on page one,
picture on page three,
had a nice ring.

The neighbors were impressed.
And he was recognized at Eastville Hardware,
picking up a can of green marine paint.
The cashier stared at him, squinting.
"Weren't you in the paper for something?"

"Why, yes.
Name on page one,
picture on page three."

"Hmmm. Surprised they let you make bail."

Adonis at Seventy-Three

His wife's figure drawing class required a model.
The instructor inquired. He assented.
His wife professed embarrassment, blushed,
then she too assented.

He had never done this before,
but assumed it entailed the ability to be still,
to do nothing for extended periods of time.
At this he excelled. (You should see him in a hammock.)

He had not misled himself.
The drawing teacher arranged his body,
told him what expression to wear,
to stare at the upper left corner of the door
for twenty minutes, break for five, and repeat.

Did I mention he got paid?
Well, it surprised him too.
Especially when he realized
that, having been paid, he had arrived.
He was now a Professional Model.

Later he chanced to mention this,
modestly, in passing,
spicing up his performance
at the Clam Shack's open mic,
underscoring <u>professional</u>
with a casual snap of his suspenders.

The men bought him a beer,
and asked how much he made.
He curtly informed them
professionals do not discuss their fees,
that their curiosity was vulgar, and mercenary.

The women asked if he posed nude.
He had long suspected
women still viewed him with sexual intent,
but was nice to have it confirmed.

Though he was puzzled
his wife had never mentioned this.

Donnie's Guitar

It's Friday, close to midnight.
Donnie bends over his guitar like a wino
cradling his last bottle of Mad Dog 20/20,
stroking it gently before he twists the seal
and settles into satisfied despair.

He works his hand low on the Martin's neck
where the frets hide high silver tones,
closes his eyes, twists his mouth,
and tortures the strings with gentle mercy
until soft blue notes slither across the room
looking for a heart to break.

The table of secretaries from First Capital Bank
has been waiting all week for Donnie
to make them feel sad and wanton.
They ask the waitress what he drinks.

"Ice tea," she says. "He really likes his tea."
The ladies have been sending it over all night.
Maybe it will loosen him up.
Maybe one of them will get lucky.

They're thinking Long Island Tea,
four shots to the glass,
and damn he's knocking it back.

But Donnie's tea comes from China,
Sri Lanka, when he's feeling loose.

For his last set he switches to his Dobro,
not a Gibson-come-lately
but the real inverted cone deal,
a model 76 from 1933.

The secretaries say it moans
like a woman in pain,
a real special kind of pain.

He finishes with "Terraplane Blues",
pops the mike into his pocket,
his Dobro and Martin into their cases

and, while the ladies plot their move,
disappears like tears in the wind,
leaving the secretarial table
a little drunk, a little frustrated.

He'll be back tomorrow night,
ready to play.

So will the secretaries.

Cleopatra Cleavage

Did they have a stable of such women,
each age appropriate to their prey?
Was she the one they trotted out
for middle aged men
nudging up against old,
desperate to avoid time's embrace?

She leaned forward across the table
spilling forth the bountiful benefits
of an extended warranty in quivering detail.

Fetched me coffee. Moved her chair
and slid her slit skirted thigh
against my denim clad leg
while she described undercoating.
How they would probe and spray
deep into the hidden and vulnerable
nether parts of my new Ford Ranger.

Edged closer, her left breast
casually brushing against my right bicep.
Her in house financing
had so much more to offer me
than my loyal, but, admit it,
pitifully drab credit union.

I was not the man she sought.
I have not nudged up, afraid,
against the hard border of age.
I have trampled it down
like the mole tunnels in my lawn,
not out of anger or malice,
but because I didn't notice them
in my hurry to mow the grass
before the rain started.

Not only have I embraced time,
I've been known to stick my tongue in her ear,
take her for a spin around the room on occasion,
dancing the Mephisto Waltz.
My wife doesn't mind.
She knows the last dance is hers.

I could have told Cleopatra Cleavage all this.

Also to use a little less make up.
Too much makes her fine crow's feet
stand out coarse and bold at the end of a day.
And how a colorful silk scarf around the neck
could shade her age toward a believable thirty-nine.
And to ease off on the perfume, please.

Instead I just said, "No thank you."

She muttered a word when she left.
I quite didn't catch it. (When you're my age
the hearing's half shot.)
But it was short, fricative, of one syllable,
ending in a hard consonant.

Life After Death

Andrew has a simple creed.
"Death is it. There is no life after…
That's why we call it death."

James tells of vivid dreams of his father,
decades dead,
dreams in which he talks to his father,
asks and follows his advice,

counsel that is generally sound.
Although in death, as in life,
his dad is occasionally wrong.

"My dreams are real."

Andrew picks up a book,
"*Moby Dick* is real,
but it's not true."

"But it is," James asserts,
and proceeds to tell the tale of the Essex
and her death at the hands of a great white whale.

"Whales don't have hands."

They argue with such intensity,
I suspect they think
their opinions matter.

Carneys Before the Dawn

It's the last night of a ten day stand.
When the marks clear the gate,
ride lights will die, cotter pins pull free,
power cords thick as anacondas
slither back onto table sized spools.

Come dawn the carneys are gone.
Flat folded Tilt-A-Whirl and Ferris wheel,
anonymous jumbles of bright metal,
flying down the road on flatbeds
to a new town with money still in its pocket.

The shining carnival is twice vanished,
like cotton candy swiped from a child
by a raiding raccoon outrunning tears
and the chaos of shouts and anger
in a chittering humpbacked sprint.

He will stop to wash his gaudy dinner
on the bank of the stream
separating fairgrounds from woods,
only to see it vanish in a pink swirl,
gone, like carneys racing before the dawn.

A Violin Played

"A fiddle is a violin played out of outdoors."
I remember that line from a poem
my sister gave me to read
when she lived in Somerset House.

A friend of hers wrote it.
Once on a visit when we returned
to her apartment she said,
"That was her, on the elevator,
the woman who wrote the poem
you admire so much."

I wondered at the delayed identification,
felt slighted by the skipped introduction.

I was still drinking then,
the kind of brother you tolerated,
but did not introduce to friends.

I hid my disappointment
under another Heineken.

The poem quoted is "WHAT IS A FIDDLE" by Rhea L. Cohen, from her chapbook, *Time of Two Lights*.

The Vatic Frog

That damn frog is staring at me again.
I don't know why I put up with him.
He just sits there, digesting my dimes,
giving me the hairy eyeball and smirking.
       He's up to something.
       I can tell.
He's an ugly thing
with a hollow back
          (I should have put a plant in
          instead of pocket change)
              and warts
               (Big ugly ones.)
He tries to bite my hand
when I borrow money for the laundromat.
       He steals from me.
       I've seen him do it.
I've lain awake
night after night
          and finally I caught him.
Oh it was difficult.
             He's crafty that frog.
Late at night when
             he thinks I'm asleep
he jumps down from the wall
and goes through my pockets.

Might as well be married.

Rejection Letter
From Dr. Seuss's Publisher

We hope you are not averse
to a rejection framed in verse.
It's not that we're perverse,
we've just never seen a poem worse.

What you were thinking of
to write a poem about love?
Did inspiration come from above
cooing like a turtledove?

What echoes of antique time
inflamed your fevered mind
with such tortured rhyme?
Or was it just too much wine?

Many have placed a starfish on the beach,
and found their love sweet as a peach.
But to have rhymed them both with leech,
we find a bit too far to reach.

We know two men who publish prose.
We like them not. We think them foes.
If it's not too much, you don't suppose,
that you could send your work to those.

Trust

I don't trust
anyone who begins or ends
a sentence with "Trust me."

any prince from,
or currently residing in,
Nigeria.

anyone who says "Y'all"
when I'm the only other
person in the room.

anyone at my front door
with a message for me
from Jesus Christ.

anyone who knows
how I should vote,
if I really love my country.

anyone whose last name
begins with a double f,
both lower case.

or anybody
who eats popcorn
with a spoon.

**On First Looking Into
Pogo's Ten Everlovin' Blue Eyed Years**

I carry a paper sack
        to put my footprints in
as I wander around the earth.

        If I've been here before
        I'd rather not know it.

It necessitates walking backwards
        but over the years
        I've grown accustomed to this.

        Acquired the knack
        you might say
        of looking forward over my shoulder
        every other step.

I'll admit it seemed strange at first,
        looking forward over my shoulder,
but how else could I pick up my footprints?

I like a lot of milk in my coffee

It's my custom to start a pot brewing
and in the interval select a large cup
half fill it with milk, take it to the microwave
and nuke it for thirty seconds.

But today, as I step to the counter
with half a mug of two percent,
the panel displays not the time,
but sixteen. Sixteen pale green seconds.

This has happened before.
I, or my wife, pull out something
a trifle early and fail to touch clear,

choosing to let time hang,
postponing dismissal,
and think nothing of it.

Should I think something of it?
Does this merit consideration?

What will become
of these orphaned seconds
when I touch clear?

Will they be reassigned?
Given some other task?
Or are they wiped out of existence?

When I touch clear,
will I kill time, just a little bit?
Trim sixteen seconds
from the lifespan of the cosmos?

And how many microwaves are there,
their timelines kited out against the universe,
patiently, bit by bit, reeling in the end times?

In a spasm of decision I press clear,
then numbers,
thirty seconds worth.

I bring two bibles to the table,
New Jerusalem and Revised Standard,
and, while my coffee sits and cools,
search Daniel, Revelations and Second Thessalonians.

I know others, Major Keyhoe, Erich von Däniken and the like,
have examined scripture and found UFOs
in Elijah's assumption and Ezekiel's visions
and high voltage transmitters in the arc of the covenant.

Be that as it may,
I find no microwaves in holy writ,
lurking about, precursing the eschaton,
though Elijah's cook off with the priests of Ba'al
does suggest a lightning bolt.

I feel a better. But would it hurt me
to make thirty seconds the hard way?

To use up the sixteen seconds
and then key in fourteen more?
Sixteen and fourteen make thirty,
and isn't there is enough risk in the world?

The Genealogy of Hotdogs

There was a brand his mother used to buy
decades ago in his Watertown childhood.
He's never been able to find it,
but he remembers the taste
and Nathan's matches it pretty well.

The right mustard is important;
"Classic Yellow" they call it now.
Back then it was just French's.
Celery salt brings it to perfection,
his grandmother's contribution,
the tale sown into the fabric of family lore.

Back in the roaring twenties she hung around
the Jefferson County Fair hotdog stand
lurking, spying, until she found the difference,
celery seed, ground to fine powder
and sifted into the plain yellow mustard.

The buns should be lightly toasted,
soft and yielding under delicate crispness.
The franks fried in an iron skillet,
gently in butter, never more than two at time.

A third would cool
before consumption,
diminishing its flavor.

Mustard and celery salt laid out with the table setting,
buns warm from the oven at its lowest heat,
and two dogs from the skillet
assemble into perfection in seconds.

Three, sometimes four, times a week,
he dines in the company of his youth.

Eastern Shore Traffic Jam

Heading off the neck in my Ranger pickup,
Food Lion bound, I get stuck in traffic.
White commercial van heading in,
grey PVC pipes strapped down tight overhead.
Dusty burgundy Chevy king cab headed out,
sixteen foot lengths of Yellow Tag pine
two by fours crowding its cargo rack.
The wood bends a bit, rising in the middle,
reaching out behind the truck to droop,
a soft bobble signaling a recent stop.

Two oversized men lean out their windows
one hand on the wheel, the other gesturing,
George and Zak, father and son,
two thirds of Annon Construction,
builders of half the last decade's houses
here on Wilsonia Neck and savior
to any neighbor with a sudden roof leak,
burst pipe or sagging floor.
They're settling something,
today's work or tomorrow's fishing.

I get out, reach over to stifle the last sway
of the lumber as I pass. It's fishing.
The cobia are in. Charles nailed one,
past the bar at the drop-off
where the channel cuts through.
Caught him on bunker he got off Tim,
our local waterman, source of good bait
and sound information, both free.
We make plans. Note tides. Ponder winds.
Heads nod at the corners of our triangle.

A bright blue SUV comes up fast, heading in,
slides behind George's van, breaking hard at the last.
Zak shakes his head, "Jersey plates. Must be visiting."

"Or lost as hell" I counter.
"Missed the turn for Bayside.
Done it myself."

George hitchhikes his thumb
over his shoulder at the car.
"Either way, he's in a hurry."

They fire up and are moving
before I'm in my cab.
In the rear view I watch Jersey plates
swerve around George's van
and fishtail through the curve.
If he's visiting, he'll be there soon.

And if he's lost, he'll loop around,
double back without knowing it,
and pass me before I get to the highway.

I'll bet he misses the Bayside turn again.
Bet two dollars.

October's Dance

In October bounty and death stride the field together.
Whistling a tune, they spin the grey thread of fall,
dancing as they weave ashen days into a cloak of bleak nights
spreading over winter to yoke autumn to spring,
linking rotting jack-o'-lantern to the sweet waking sap
rushing through snow, singing maple leaf to pale sylvan jade.

Let Us Go Then You and I

Let us roll up our jeans,
present a broad pale blue stripe
hovering above our ankles
advertising our delinquent intent
to porch bound town elders
sipping their second cup of coffee.

While they postpone their day,
we shall slide between tan dunes,
slip down the dew damp path
to stride the wet edge of Meteor Beach,
remnant of Appalachian glory
perched on centuries of wind and rain.

We'll join children digging castle moats
hoping to lure back the ebbing tide
as they crenellate walls with dribbled sand
chiseled from the eons by turgid rivers
sliding down diminished summits
to rest at the bottom of geology's hill.

We will leap peaks with every casual step
while waves lap once-were highlands
and whisper of eminent mortality,
the mockery of mountains worn smooth
falling on ears deafened by morning sun,
the company of children too young to fear time.

Matawoman Flats

The tide washes muddy sand
from between his toes.
When it reaches his ankles
he'll shoulder his rake,
brace the basket on his hip
like a mother and child,
and splash his way
to home and friends.

However many clams he has
will have to do for today.
Tomorrow is another tide.

Chuck Willow

Outside my window
the chuck willow sings the sun up,
pulls light from the night,
makes day out of dark.

She will return long hours later,
bid the heated summer day rest,
pull grey light down from of the sky,
sing me to bed.

Sing me to sleep,
dreaming of a muttering dawn,
a chuck willow's ragged song
outside my window.

Monarch of All She Surveys

The monarch flutters inside her globular world,
but a yard in radius, the limit of her vision.
Yet she finds our three plant milkweed plot,

set midst a vinca ground clutter,
over towered by a maze of rosemary,
day lilies, and rampant japonica.

Finds it with the wily surety
of a politician, glad hand out,
plucking votes from a crowd.

Winter Kingfisher

A belted kingfisher swoops
and dips along the shore
seeking a minnow breakfast,
his white vest flashing
like the thin clear ice,
shattered and scattered,
drifting out from the reeds.

Hard times, he chitters.
Where are the killifish of summer?

First Fire

I choose a warmish day
for the stove's first fire.
Set the window exhaust fan
to draw off the funeral smoke
of summer's spiders and webs
mixed with last July's coat of paint
baking off its final fumes.

The cats gather,
gluttons for warm,
calico and tuxedo
disciples of the stove.

Flames crackle behind the glass,
But only feed me wood,
and I will give you summer
all your winter long.

Ax and Wood

Red oak jumps apart
at the first strike,
tumbles from the block
in bisected humility.

Cherry calls for more force.
It generally complies,
except when twisted in the grain.
Then it's a contest of will.

And though I've always won,
it's always been a struggle,
the moral victory
going to the wood.

Wood Heat

My friend heats with wood. Hunts trees.
He prowls in his predatory pickup,
circling the grove, seeking the weak,
the wind toppled, the standing dead.

When the power crew's out,
clearing the line of tree and limb,
he alters his route home
and gleans half a cord.

A good man to know after a nor'easter.
He cuts and trims the downed pine,
leaving a nest of green-needled slash,
and jacks the long logs into a border for your drive.
Oak, maple and such, simply disappear into his truck,
even to the small branches. Kindling.

His doctor told him, "Join a gym or kiss your heart goodbye."
He bought a Fisher Stove, an axe and a chainsaw.
A lightning scarred butternut by the front porch went first.
He left a stump three feet tall, and near as wide, for splitting.

He splits and ricks two winters ahead,
and after that sells it by the pickup load,
delivered and stacked right on your porch.
He doesn't need the money, but the yard is only so big.

Don't get him started on wood.
Mrs. Browning never wrote
as he speaks of wood.
Let him count the ways.

Maple shatters as much as splits.
Red oak splits clean, but white will work you.
The difficulty of beech and gum
is made small by cutting to a short length.

Hickory is tough, but well worth it.
The bark leaps off at the splitting,
giving you fire wood and fire starter,
all in one blow.

Locust can go from axe to fire,
but burns cleaner,
and smells sweeter,
given two months on the porch.

There's nothing like dogwood.
It dies standing up, seasons in place,
gives up a heat that shames birch
and endures beyond hickory.
He saves it for the bitter nights.

Oh, and don't get him started on fire.
Twigs, a pine cone, (and one only)
sprinkled with cedar shavings,
tightly curled for choice,
followed by split birch,
makes for a hot start.

Add oak, first red, then white,
for lasting flame and a bed of coals.
Top it off with hickory,
as much as the stove will hold.

Put a full kettle on the trivet,
(keeps the water from boiling off)
and damp the fire back.
Warms a house the whole night through.

Open the damper at dawn,
refill the kettle and set it next to the flue.
You've a roaring fire in half a minute,
and hot water for coffee in two.

He cooks on that thing.
His food is greasy,
when it's not burnt.
The coffee's bitter.
He sweetens it with maple syrup.

Drop by some time.
He'll be glad to see you.
Just don't ask about wood
or how to build a fire.

Punctuation

The semicolon is on life support,
living in a muted twilight,
like the umlaut, kept half alive
by the dogged but slowly descending brow
of *The New Yorker*.

Oh, I spotted an umlaut or two in *Foreign Affairs*.
But that was decades ago,
and I only subscribed because I was drunk,
the price and title deceiving me.
I thought I was ordering porn.
(It did come in a plain brown wrapper.)

But the semicolon is not an umlaut
loitering about *The New Yorker,*
puffing on a vowel,
the correct pronunciation of coöperation
dangling from the corner of its mouth.
No one has ever *heard* a semicolon.

No. The semicolon is on the way out.
Its passing will go unmourned,
save by very few. My elder sister
and English teachers come to mind,
perhaps a few librarians, but no one else.

Not so the hardy hyphen.
He's everywhere these days
right in the middle of a six-pack.
And when did that happen?

Did they think when I stopped drinking beer
they could slam a hyphen
right in the middle of every six-pack?
Apparently. Because they damn sure did.

Used to be, you bought a six-pack
and drank it in a week or an hour,
the can went in one bin, snap ring in another.
I don't recall recycling any hyphens.
And don't tell me it was the beer.

I only had the two bins.
If the six-pack had been sporting a hyphen
I would have been awash in them,
combing them out of my beard,
finding them in my soup,
clogging the dryer filter.
But it wasn't sporting a hyphen.
Not then.

Now they're everywhere,
"The young men labored
at their Eagle-Scout project,
a soon-to-be-completed
reproduction of a colonial-era-
covered-footbridge."

OK, I made that up.
But is it too much to ask for
just one bin at the recycling center.
I mean, our land-fills are overflowing.

The semicolon, for all its faults,
has a sense of modesty, of dignity.
You won't find one jammed into a six-pack.
Not ever.

If it were not so humble,
possessed a stronger sense of self-worth,
even self-preservation,
perhaps things would be different.

But alas, the semicolon will fade away,
its lone memorial the uncorrected typo,
the funeral sparsely attended.
I'll be there, supporting my weeping sister.
But I won't really care. No one will.

Quotidian

You might have surmised that quotidian
had something to do with quotations.
Presumed, perhaps, that quotidian
meant someone who quotated a lot,
incessantly, perhaps obnoxiously.

There he goes again, quoting
Marlowe, Spencer and Shakespeare
in one long drawn out sentence.
The worst part is, that he got it right.
God, what an insufferable quotidian.

You might think that.
But you'd be wrong.
And no, I won't tell you.
You'll have to look it up.

Mixology

Do not mix your metaphors.

Oh, but I have. I have.
I have mixed them with
my favorite finger of speech,
and written them in ink
that cannot be erased.

I have buttered my bed
and now must lie upon it.

How to Study a Poem

If the ink is dry, read it.
If the ink is not dry, wait a bit.

[Hint: If the poem is in a book,
the ink is dry and it is safe to proceed.]

When you look it over for the first time,
read only the words present for duty.
Ignore the others, the ones in your head,
but not on the page.

[Hint: The words on the page appear against their will.
The poet did not consult them, or the ones he left out.
Do not be confused. Words are not the victim here.]

Run through the poem again
and ponder its meaning.
Does it make you feel happy?
Then it's a happy poem.
Does it make you feel confused?
Then you are stupid, or the poet is.
Let's blame the poet.

[Hint: If poet is in the room with you,
don't worry about his feelings.
Tell him to leave. Be firm about this.]

If the last hint seems cruel, consider,
if a frog had pockets in his vest,
he'd require origami skills to fold a letter
from his mother small enough to it put away.
When he took it out, he would find
the creases had rendered it illegible.

[Hint: This is the frog's problem. Not yours.]

I have been less than honest.
When I told you it was safe to proceed,
I lied. Poetry is never safe.

I also said, *Words are not the victim here*,
and you probably inferred the poet was.
Not so. You are.

Finally, frogs don't have vests,
or pockets in them. They do have wings.
However, they are vestigial,
too small to support them in flight.
Which is why every time a frog jumps,
he bumps his butt.

Good luck with the poem.
I'll be in the next room.

**Last Note
On a Unicorn's Horn**

Bestiaries and Arthurian tales,
I searched these.

Constructed the awkward verse
of early manhood's first opened eyes.

Linked its spiraled horn
to my oughts and shoulds.

Sought to stand as the wild Celt
with his shrieking discophonant horn
ripped from the wild kine.

Sought to stand on the eagle's crag

between earth and sky
between water and fire
and with one clear spiraling note
encircle the world.

    And never once counted the cost
    of getting such a horn.

Ken Sutton is not crazy. But he does have voices in his head, old men and children, friends and enemies, close relatives and people who waited with him at a bus stop in 1966. They have something to say, an act to justify, a sorrow to share, a moment of awe that overcame them in the event and still does in memory, or just the prettiest damn thing they ever saw.

Up on my ladder, cleaning the gutters when sixteen swans flew over, muttering soft calls, wings stroking through air like a swimmer in no hurry and one snow goose, mute, wings beating like a claw hammer banjo to keep up, and doing it, holding its place in the V-line making for the fields on the other side of the neck.

There's a poem in that. But don't trust the pronoun. It might have happened to him, a neighbor who looked up raking her yard, or he might have overheard two watermen over coffee at the Machipongo Trading Co.

He has lived in a variety of states, New York (upstate), Texas, Massachusetts, Louisiana, and, since 1986, Virginia. He retired in 2012 and lives near Machipongo on the Eastern Shore of Virginia with Carolyn, his wife of long and patient standing. He wrote poetry in his youth. Good poetry, he was told. He took it back up when the flurry of his retirement settled down.

Peg Volk, host of the Great Machipongo Clam Shack's open mic dubbed him the Bard of Machipongo in 2013 and he has been haunting the open mics of the Eastern Shore and Hampton Roads under that name since.

Ken is on the advisory board for the Poetry Society of Virginia. His two future books of poetry, *The Midrash of the Marginal*, and *The Convenience of War*, are nearing completion.

colophon

Brought to you by Wider Perspectives Publishing, care of Tanya Cunningham-Jones and James Wilson with the mission of advancing the poetry and creative community of Hampton Roads, Virginia.

See our production of the works of
- Tanya Cunningham (Scientific Eve)
- Ray Simmons
- Taz Waysweete'
- Bobby K. (The Poor Man's Poet)
- J. Scott Wilson (TEECH!)
- Jorge Mendez & JT Williams
- Lisa Kendrick
- Sarah Eileen Williams
- Ken Sutton

Stephanie Diana (Noftz)
and others to come soon.

> *We promote and support the artists of the 757*
> *from the seats, from the stands,*
> *from the snapping fingers and clapping hands*
> *from the pages, and the stages*
> *and now we pass them forth to the ages*
>
> *(Stop it James, just stop it!)*

Seek the above artists on FaceBook, the Virginia Poetry Online channel on YouTube, and the Hampton Roads Artistic Collective webpage. Hampton Roads Artistic Collective is the non-profit extension of WPP and strives to simultaneously support worthy causes in Hampton Roads and the creative artists.

Ken may be reached at

Ken Sutton
P.O. Box 81
Machipongo, VA 23405

Made in the USA
Middletown, DE
04 October 2024